LAST POEMS

LAST POEMS

DOUGLAS HOUSTON

Shoestring Press

Printed by imprintdigital
Upton Pyne, Exeter
www.imprintdigital.com

Typeset and cover design by narrator
www.narrator.me.uk
info@narrator.me.uk
033 022 300 39

Published by Shoestring Press
19 Devonshire Avenue, Beeston, Nottingham, NG9 1BS
(0115) 925 1827
www.shoestringpress.co.uk

First published 2016
© Copyright: Douglas Houston

Cover illustration by Manon Houston

The moral right of the author has been asserted.

ISBN 978-1-910323-35-9

Donation

ACKNOWLEDGEMENTS

Shoestring Press is immensely grateful to Lynne Houston, the poet's widow, for making available the text of the poems included in *Last Poems*, some of which celebrate the intense happiness of their relationship and marriage.

The press is also grateful to Sean O'Brien for permission to reprint his poem, 'The Wendigo'.

To his children
Whom he loved with a passion
For Sam, Iggy, Lloyd, Manon
With Love

CONTENTS

INTRODUCTION

Reading these *Last Poems* by Douglas Houston, we might be forgiven for imagining their author wrote them with some anticipation of their position at the end of his life's work. These are poems haunted by lost opportunities, acutely conscious of the passing of wasted time. Their prevailing tone is one of resignation and amusement at whatever cosmic joke the world seems intent on seeing through. There's a bleakness often broken, like the typical Houston weather of grey skies and drizzling cold, by 'absolute light', by a surprising warmth, by unexpected glimpses of mysterious beauty or some sense of the glorious absurdity of everything, just before the darkness and drizzle close in once more:

> Lying half-awake in the weather particular
> To its chosen treasure, regret wonders
> Why the clock is ticking so loudly
> And why the ticks come in such quick succession.

['The Weather Regrets']

Neat as it might seem to think of these poems as somehow conscious of their own finality, however, the truth is that this same tone is already present in the earliest poems included in Houston's 1986 debut collection, *With The Offal Eaters,* published when he was 39, following years of experimentation with the lifestyles and poetics of the post-sixties counter-culture. *With The Offal Eaters* was a belated consolidation of the mature voice Houston first announced in the pages of Douglas Dunn's *A Rumoured City: New Poets From Hull* (1982), a signature blend of realist detail and outlandish extrapolation, firmly grounded in the textures of life without money in the provincial hinterlands.

Soon after publishing a review of *With The Offal Eaters* in *Poetry Wales*, I discovered that Houston and I were near neighbours. He and his second family – the painter Karen

Pearce and their two children, Lloyd and Manon, with occasional visits from Sam and Iggy, Houston's two sons from a previous marriage – were living in Cwmbrwyno, a small cluster of houses, abandoned lead mines and fields of sheep just a mile or two from my own rented house near Ponterwyd, among the hills through which the inland road from Aberystwyth winds its way along a mountain pass towards Llangurig. This landscape informed much of his second book, *The Hunters In The Snow* (1994), and following our introduction the poetry became indelibly connected with the memorable presence of Houston himself.

How to describe him? He was, I suppose, almost exactly what he appears to be in his poems: a character shaped by his family's experience of the Second World War who had gone on to embrace the social convulsions of the 1960s and 1970s and emerge, in the aftermath of the Miners' Strike, as a curious hybrid of protestant respectability, David Niven-style charm and erudition, and sociable hang-dog semi-dereliction. His ability to generate a kind of amiable chaos even while engaged in such small actions as making a cup of tea or finding a book on his own shelves was near-legendary, matched only by his ability to remain unfazed by whatever extraordinary situation might be unfolding around him.

In the poems, this combination of old school charm and heightened awareness of absurdity are qualities that mark his voice as distinctive. Houston's thoughts – by turns particular and philosophical, documentary-confessional and deadpan surreal – emerge from a consciousness that is without vanity, processing exactly-noted details through a very grounded metaphysical perspective. In the meditations on marital breakdown, Wittgenstein's philosophy and mountain-climbing that made up much of his third collection, *The Welsh Book of the Dead* (2000), Houston's poems worry insistently at "questions that always evaded language" with no expectation of finding definitive answers.

The publication of these *Last Poems*, following the uncollected material gathered in *Beyond The Playing Fields: New & Selected Poems* (2010), mean that Houston's body of work, published at a rate of roughly one book for each decade of his career, curiously mirrors that of Philip Larkin, whose presence as university librarian in Hull during his student years was always something of a touchstone, even as W.H. Auden and his own first-hand experience of the long decline of the counter-culture were more immediate and deeper influences on the poems he came to write. Even so, it's arguable that one consistent aspect of Houston's work lies in its reconciliation of a kind of Larkinesque melancholia with some aspects of European decadence and the *poète maudit* strains of Baudelaire and Rimbaud:

> Absinthe, while the moon wanes, east of a garden
> With square-trimmed hedges eight feet high.
> The man enters his shed...

['Farnham']

Quite unlike Larkin, however, we also find an ongoing preoccupation with philosophy (Wittgenstein being the key figure in Houston's thinking), a commitment to domesticity and a Zen-like grounding in the moment, all contained by a wry self-awareness that manages to be often at odds, but never quite out of love, with the world it inhabits and the people it moves among:

> The going's easy in a city
> as flat and equable as water,
> slow and green in the light through trees,
> that lets you sit and smoke, watch drifting swans
> for half-an-hour, to advise against
> missing the point of the present tense.

['Amsterdam']

Houston's poems also sketch a distinct political landscape, his scenarios often simultaneously post-apocalyptic and semi-feudal, inhabited by a voice that speaks up for the forgotten places of semi-rural Britain, eking out its days alongside those on the receiving end of de-industrialisation, who get by on precarious work with only the most threadbare means of survival.

This reality was essentially Houston's own life, whose circumstances regularly swung between periods of domestic contentment and financial instability, much as his poems shift gears between fleeting pleasures, natural sublimity and satirical visions of privatised abandonment or decay.

Throughout Houston's body of work, psychedelic hallucinations and the trappings of folklore are often embedded in factually drawn scenes: even in these *Last Poems*, a witch might still predict a coming hurricane by reading the entrails of dogs under a bridge, or a sinister woodland consume an unwary traveller. Always the freelance, with a permanently unsettled present and uncertain future, it's telling that while these *Last Poems* emerged from one of Houston's less tumultuous personal phases, settled into a happy fourth marriage with Lynne in Huddersfield, for the poems themselves any sense of contentment remains a brittle and contingent thing.

Re-reading Houston's poetry now, with the implausible cold fact of his absence in mind, it strikes me that he inhabits his own work in much the same way the first-person narrators of Spanish picaresque novels like *Lazarillo de Tormes* occupied the roads they travelled through the corrupt and insecure world of the sixteenth and seventeenth centuries. These *Last Poems* may mark an ending of sorts, but it's characteristic that even Houston's most mordant reflections ultimately refuse any sense of finality and keep faith, as always, with the present tense:

> Here comes England, with its fraying flags
> Clipped to the Ford's back doors
> And the cut-price Carling from the cash-and-carry
> On the Wootton Bassett trading estate.
>
> The absolute light on the cherry tree
> Blossoming above its neglected patch
> Gets lost in the purple twilight
> And disappears for days into thin rain.

['June 2010']

Wayne Burrows

THE WENDIGO

i.m. Douglas Houston

You would have recognized this place,
The path that runs beside the Metro, walked
By sober adults and their upright dogs
But turning into bandit country
Now the nights draw in at just gone three.
The wire fences like the ones at school
Seem placed to emphasize the ragged edge
Of a forsaken order we affected to despise –
Mundane municipalities that could afford
To house and feed our discontent. No more.
Where once the Wild Wood grew, the in-between
Emerges as a bleak and Badgerless republic,
Hawthorn scrub and sycamore, and on a lost
Allotment bordering a siding and a tunnel
Fireweed staggers on like wild white-headed Lears.
You would have understood this place
Speaks only with itself, and yet have tried
To overhear the rumour of the shoaling leaves
And cider-bottles, rutted earth and Durex
And, concealed among the red-raw docks,
Discreet excreta of the (canine?) bourgeoisie.
What does it say, this nightfall then, with
Everyone indoors or meant to be, as darkness
Takes possession of the ground once more
Or waits impatiently beyond the flickering rim
Of failing streetlight? You must know by now.
There comes the howl of the disconsolate
Exurban Wendigo, who cannot be appeased
By knowing he does not exist. Ah Wendigo,
The case is worse for those who must be real.

Sean O'Brien

The Wendigo is a Native American mythological figure, and there's a famous
horror story by Algernon Blackwood called 'The Wendigo'. In this case I
leave out the sinister side of the creature to focus on his untamed nature

WELCOME BACK

for Lynne

Though days apart are drab and bare,
My hearts glad that you are there
When thoughts from you come through
To warm me with the fact you care,
Though winter gathers in the air,
And days bring nothing new.

So welcome home my DarLynne one,
From out there in the spanish sun.
Relax and tell me all.
Enjoy the chocs. There just to say
Each day with you's a holiday
Whatever might befall.

INTRUDER

I could never find my way back there now,
To a bend on a thin road in the hills
Where the land is bare but for rough stone walls
And thorn trees crippled by the wind.
Three miles away below the western sky
The Teifi meandered in its mild vale
Where my parents lived and now they're buried,
Rich pastures where the trees grow straight.
Up there were only the last-ditch sheep farms,
Improbable, isolated dwellings
And corrugated iron dilapidations
Fixed to their outcrop-studded fields.
I don't remember why I'd stopped, stepped out
Of the van I'd been aimlessly driving
Distracted by solitude and movement
From the void of that afternoon.
The little house's only door was open,
Tucked in a corner where the roof slopes met
And broken slates stacked in the gutter meant
Neglect, even abandonment.
The kitchen was a 1950s set-piece
With its chequered oilcloth on the table,
The wooden draining board and antique stove
Offering no signs of recent use.
The cupboards held flour crusted with green mould,
Tea and beef stock cubes with packet designs
That looked decades out of date. In a drawer
I found a large gold pocket watch.
I took two pairs of gold cuff links as well
And a pretty brooch in pinchbeck and jet.
Transgression, trespass, and eerie desertion
Got me away without delay.
Next morning insisted on cancelling
The plan to sell the things. I forced myself
To knock upon the door I'd closed and wait
Till fear sank into the silence.

No breath of change inside as I replaced
The loot, watched only by the emptiness
That allowed the light to approve my decision,
My hope no one had been disturbed.

AMSTERDAM

for Paul Evans

The North Sea mist is the aerosol rain
that alternates with the mid-June sun,
so it's humid and your clothes are wrong
for the walking that goes on and on
when you're lost and guess the way's along
the next long straight of cobbles and canal.

The season and weather were the same
fifty years ago when you first came
with your brother and Dad, both since dead
and drawn into shadowed perspectives
through the eyes of successive bridges,
where the ways cross and you guess again.

The going's easy in a city
as flat and equable as water,
slow and green in the light through trees,
that lets you sit and smoke, watch drifting swans
for half-an-hour, to advise against
missing the point of the present tense.

A CHILD'S HISTORY OF DEATH

i.m. G.M. Houston, 1886-1982

You can look back no further
Than the hundred-acre view
Across distances where walks
Called 'going to see Grampy'
Always ended where Nana
Went quiet and changed the flowers.

A squat black cross marked the plot,
Slightly sunk for its eight years
In the grassy tracts out past
The obelisks and angels,
The locus of the absence
Where Grampy was and wasn't.

Nana, who was always old,
Her white hair a shock of grief
Matching her widow's wardrobe,
Told you enough of the facts
Of what happened, then left them
Buried, moving on to Heaven.

More than thirty years later
You had Nana's last lesson,
First of your dead, kissing her,
As you would not the others,
Before she took the long drive
Back to where she'd left Grampy.

CUBA JIM

Your friend's from Yorkshire, the accent surviving
His years at an American school in Cuba.
Transatlantic-exotic, he speaks Spanish too.
You covet his Mexican silver knife,
Its heavy blade and turquoise-studded grip.
Big Aggy called him 'Cuba Jim', which stuck.

Teenage resident aliens in Glasgow,
You pause on your uphill walk from school,
Looking down on its buildings and playgrounds
In the gloom of October dusk on the city
At a latitude slightly north of Moscow,
Way over there, where night's well underway.

The talk's of imminent nuclear war.
You agree that direct-hit obliteration
Seems preferable to death from radiation.
The future's on hold while Kennedy and Kruschev
Go on squaring up to one another
And nobody's saying it just can't happen.

You've dreamed your family typically at home –
All settled in the customary places
On the three-piece round the coal fire and TV –
With fallout drifting down through the ceiling
In flakes like dirty snow through windless air,
Love silent in its mortal helplessness.

Cuba Jim's not impressed by Glasgow,
Where the Hoover Company sent his father
After Castro nationalized everything.
You carry on over the grass to the bus-stop
Beneath a Cold War sky charged with the threat
That's fallen on the world like winter all at once.

Then your father's moved again
In a multinational managerial shuffle.
You go to London. Cuba Jim visits.
Then phone chats, till the time the ring-tone sounds
Over hundreds of miles of December night,
And you suddenly think he might be dead.

His mother answers, can't speak when you ask for him.
He died two days ago, his father says.
Brain haemorrhage. They promise you his knife.
One comes, but it's not the Mexican blade.
You never see its like again, nor his,
This one-off waiting with you for the end.

HAPPY BIRTHDAY

Some fold their years neatly, put them away
in proper order, immaculate napkins
beyond future use, forever white
every time the big cupboard opens to show
the motes of dust that might have been people
floating on shafts of sunlight.

Most can find the years that matter,
make accurate reference to those that act
as switches for the mechanisms
on which our narratives depend.
They end up in a box in the attic,
where we sometimes rummage with a fading torch.

Each birthday adds its chip to the pile,
your all-or-nothing bet on still being here
when the wheel's turned through another year.
God may be trying to tell me something
by permitting my survival to date,
despite the waste of folly and bad habits,

to enjoy this birthday, walking with you
and our daft old dog this March morning
down the easy straights along the canal,
bright air spiked by the tips of new buds
on the abundant trees and bushes
where the annual unveiling of Spring proceeds.

DEBRIEFING

"a love that does not abandon" – W.H. Auden, 'Amor Loci'

for L.B.

Midnight approaching, silence, peace,
Beyond the months of disconnection.
You sense the future's howling's eased,
While *Forward* stays the one direction
Over the rubble and through the waste
Of *might have been* and mad distraction.
You're past the shock of your release,
And steadier now after defection
From what you wished for that backfired,
The smoke stream rising from hot coals
That got you higher than required,
Your tin-lid crucible burning holes
In some escape plan that expired
In loss of plot that singed your soul.
The crash-landing went off all right,
All things considered. Pause for thought:
An end to smoking through the night
Snapped at by dogs of *must* and *ought* –
A fair swap for prescription stuff
That puts you back in touch again,
Slowing you down, if not enough
To pass for 24-carat sane –
Who does? Normality is tough.
We all need help to take the strain.
The poor die first when the going's rough
And a pale horse wakes and shakes his mane,
While maniacs in love with power
With mates next door who sell them tanks
Push chaos further by the hour
And throw more cash in empty banks
To keep the savage farce on stage.
There's a decent chance that you can cope

On the borders of advancing age,
Being blessed with her whose love and hope
Survive beside you and assuage
Some empty ache that's eased by dope
In terror as the world grows old
And desperate winters no less cold.

DIURNALITY

Very late, or too early for light,
night's pointless watches often find you
propped by the elbows on the bookcase
in the darkness that becomes the fact
that you're older than ever before.

Back in bed beside her who sleeps on,
the last of consciousness disperses
in praise of Utter Comfort, Its warmth
in the soft fit of body, mattress,
duvet, woman, pillows, and darkness.

Faint high frequencies of the first birds
twitter in the imperfect silence
of tinnitus' stratospheric whine
and resonant arpeggios start
with pale light seeping into the sky.

Day is the long passage of waking,
sixteen hours or thereabouts standard,
in the freedom from being useful
that comes with the bus pass and pension
and gets you through till the night shift starts.

DUSK

Night's already seeping from the screen
Of boughs and briars the fence can't contain
At the western end of the pub car park,
Where the kids can practice swearing undisturbed
And nothing marks where the loser died
In a fight that happened before they were born.

Later, they're down by the canal,
Water spurting aerated jets
Through cracks in the black lock gates.
Somebody's drunken uncle drowned here
The last time he took the short-cut home.

You have watched the generations inherit
Their patterns of years in the weave of this place
Where your own threads run their brighter strands.
Dear woman, hold my hand, please, while the sun
Is setting on all this living and dying
Brought hot to the anvil of days.

ECCLESIASTES

The old man who says it's going to rain
is invariably right before long
where days are a dull documentary
about conditions in abandoned mines
with patches of sunshine for remission
when back gardens open on how it should be.

Vexation amuses him, its devices
and mechanisms witty inventions
whose movements he watches impassively
as he leans on a neighbour's gate to rest
and make lewd remarks to shame her vanity
on his way through the world as far as the shop.

He disarms offence with the routine smile
kept in the thicket of his hair-cowled face,
wisdom and madness and folly alike
of no concern while he's on good terms
with his patient terminal illness
and finds no reason for giving a damn.

No fuss, then, when he slips away
sitting on the sofa watching TV
while his mate is making a cup of tea
and he doesn't care when he turns up late
in the flashiest hearse in town
to join those gathered for the burning.

EQUINOCTIAL

When the year knows its better half's done,
 Dark comes in cold through the rain curtain
Whose every spattering drop is a beat
 In the drumming below the clatter
Where flagstones catch what blocked gutters spill.

Over there, the bodies are buried
Under briars in the thigh-deep grass.
 Rain strikes steel-band notes from toppled urns
And night thickens where the trees grow dense
To black that throbs with the eyeballs' pulse.

Six months on and Spring is under way
 In general budding, early blossom
On the small tree where the pavement turns.
 A cuckoo with a Yorkshire accent
Flutes far off when the road is quiet,

Fitting the zodiacal moment,
 Elevated and facing the light
That fills the world and will hold until
 The time comes back round and Winter falls
In huts and on journeys along the way.

MUSCULOSKELETAL

"You learned the concept 'pain' when you learned language."
– Wittgenstein

Your bones walk you around the town
Then moan in idiolects of pain
About the hours of work they've done,
Remind you that it's tablet time again,

The stuff that dulls both misery and the brain,
Off-duty when there's call for concentration –
With anything more than lying down a strain,
You make a full-time job of managing pain.

The hairline fractures in the vertebrae,
The cracked ribs, and the muscles wired with nerves
Object to action rather strenuously,
Insist that movement only makes things worse.

Pain's lousy company, the same as you,
Monotonous and occasionally a trial.
It's all yours so the best that you can do
Is keep it to yourself. No need to smile.

REMOTE

When the hills begin, the thin road sheds
Its tall hazel hedges with fresh white wounds
Hacked by mechanical blades.
From here, there are only the tracks without signposts
That thread the plateau above the valley,
Out past the old mine's collapsed workings,
Its failed village where a few go on living
And bog-cotton stars stud the peaty drabness.

Decades since I drove here, navigation
Draws what it can from the fading half-life
Of fragments memory offers for a map
To take me through three farmyards,
With stops for the opening and closing of gates,
Slowly through flooding and over potholes,
Till a final turn confirms this is indeed the way
Back to the house where my children were young.

TROOPER WARD COMES HOME

for Baz Ward

The war is over and summer confirms
that everything's glorious. The flags are out
and the girls look good as the troopship moors
with thousands of homecoming PoWs
waving from rails in the hull's grey cliff.

Everyone's smiling in black and white,
the contrast sharp in the English light
on the Pathé news from Liverpool.
where the men coming down the long gangway
are home the moment they merge with the crowd,

and that's him – there, now! – your father,
turning smartly on his crutches
as he swings onto the quay,
minus the leg lost in Italy
to a shell from a German tank.

Click 'Play' again, re-animate that young man,
lean, dark-haired, and sharp-profiled, like you,
his future son, were at his age
decades ago when we were young with you,
Lynne and I, whose own dead fathers

step ashore by proxy, back from that war,
sole survivors of the Burmese jungle
and North Atlantic, whose memories stranded them
out past language, as we three children knew
when the shadow of their silences fell.

WEDDING MUSIC: SCHUBERT D 667

When the doors opened, we were borne on the music
To the spot where we stood and became man and wife,
The noon sky clearing through tall south-western windows
While the piano soloed the pure melody,
 Naked as sunlight striking lively spring water.

Orion climbs to morning in the eastern darkness
Where the dawn sun will float above the mist on lawns
And tidy copses that punctuate the mild sweep
Of the house's parkland to the distant limits
Of money, good taste, and centuries of privilege.

Another winter is closing in on the moors
And *together* is better for one married day
When the car radio is randomly switched on
And instantly brings coincidence's blessing –
The Trout Quintet illuminating our silence.

THE WEATHER REGRETS

The snow that fell two days before,
Not densely, but slowly in huge flakes
So white rose petals filled the dead air,
Is thawing to dirty gouts in shadows.

Winter's old and leaving its squalor
Where the garden's abandoned to rotting leaves
And damaged plastic furniture
Vanadlised by recent gales.

The weather doesn't notice you're asleep.
It goes on adjusting conditions,
Migrant air still freezing from Siberia
Or stillness that won't shift a feather on grass.

A few times a year when the darkness
Through curtains is indigo, summer
Comes in through the bedroom window
And every breath fills the lungs with sky.

Any weather's right for regret. Glum months
Suit it. Sunlit poignancy is special.
In bed, it makes long excursions
To where what might have been was last seen.

Lying half-awake in the weather particular
To its chosen treasure, regret wonders
Why the clock is ticking so loudly
And why the ticks come in such quick succession.

FARNHAM

Absinthe, while the moon wanes, east of a garden
With square-trimmed hedges eight feet high.
The man enters his shed.
Leaving his wife on the accommodating sofa.
While the lodger, with a second glass of absinthe –
Milky as moonlight, green as the garden –
Absorbs these November moments,
Their holy architecture
Of silence and solitariness,
Of the very last blooms
That will have shed their petals by morning,
Of distance from sounds of bypass and railway,
In this interval that is not death
Nor life as I must live it.
Here is neither love in its parsimony
Nor hate's profane reflexes
Whose involuntary spasms seize the language,
Just a pocket-handkerchief of garden
In last defiance of encroaching Winter,
Another glass of absinthe, and a cigarette.
The cold touch on the right of my neck
As I sit here in an unbuttoned shirt
Is the night that says 'You shall sleep
And never wake again to this moment,
Though similar diamonds may, perhaps,
Be found again in the sand of the life that is getting by'.

HURRICANE LAURA

Foreseen in the spilling of the guts of dogs
By the old witch living under the bridge,
The rumours kept on through hard winter fogs
When it got so cold we switched off the fridge
Put the grub outside in a blue plastic crate,
Though we didn't bring it in till a little too late,
And the morning when the milk went sour
The news was breaking with the first of the showers
That spun from the wheel she rolled through the sky
With that kick in the wind as it passed us by.

What we hadn't known was that she'd sought
A stopover here as some last resort.
It was 4 a.m. when the knocking came
On the good front door that your ex had bought,
Where a man worn-out beyond taking blame
Asked to come in, then added 'But
I've someone with me'. Well, that was that –
Enquire no further, straight back to bed,
Though we heard them at it, it has to be said,
And leaving her shoes was the cruellest cut.

She didn't rush, just wheeled around
Slowly out on the edges of town
Till she hit like a high-yield megaton blast.
We'd dug in deep by then, before the shock's
Invisible tsunami ripped through fast,
But life got tough in that mouldy hole
With our bags of bits and our dwindling stocks
Of the fuel hope burns in the human soul
And the months in the dark took a heavy toll
While the batteries died on all the clocks.

When we breathed the sky again that day
We felt blessed with light, though we sensed a risk –
Seemed the air had changed, the world gone damp
And breathing seemed harder in the lingering mist,
With power still rationed and routine gone
As the fells grew busy with survivors' camps
And our families scattered beneath what sun
We had that year in the dear old place,
Though our health came second in the race
Between peace and quiet and what she'd done.

THE TROPIC OF DEIGHTON

Inhale, let the smoke bloom in the bloodstream
So the world slips into neutral. Ride the surge
To a tingle that earths through the toes
Into warm concrete, where the cat is stretched
In supplication to the sun.

Sunday afternoon and custom encourages you
To do as little as you might wish. The trees grow lazy
Under the weight of all that leaf and seed.
The hours drift along their canal of air
Banked by wilderness and a red brick terrace.

Though the tea is Darjeeling, we are hardly genteel,
The ashtrays black with use, the dog shit drying
On the scrubby lawn where the visiting chickens
Stab the dirt lightly with their tiny heads.
Who are you to shrug at the arrangements?

You might enjoy retirement here, may, indeed,
Already be doing so, low-budget Horatian,
Fringed with rank vegetation where sunken car panels
Poke from the dominant briars. Smoke some more,
Pass it on. It is Sunday and this is what we do.

THE NORTH-SOUTH ROADS

These are the north-south roads, my son,
the ones we used to travel on
after your mother took you away.
A long time's gone since the holidays
when Dad turned up with the climbing gear
in an old estate with the pillows and quilts
laid out for sleeping in the rear.

Night fell in Wales up some forest track,
with nothing to pay and a good fire.
Days wore us out on summit trudges
or risking too much on steep rock ridges,
where I was glad to let you take the lead,
already stronger and more confident
than I, left joined to you by the sagging rope.

For seven years, we took the north-south roads,
a father and a son whose world
came into being by being together
on trips displacing all our separation.
As fathers do, I must have wanted you
to be like me, to know the wild places
where the streams run clear on the unfenced slopes.

Driving now down the north-south roads,
to the wilderness where your will was trained
to endurance and its rewards,
it's four years since you cut me off
for a passing marriage to comfort and cash
with a woman who didn't approve of you
and couldn't see the point of being free.

EKPHRASIS

When you are out, I look at the photographs:

You standing with the bullocks behind you,
Your smile one with the sunshine's brightness
On lush grazing and woods in the distance.

You in a minor museum,
Wearing a Roman helmet
With a wide-eyed grin
That goes straight through
The porcelain dome of heaven,
Or paying cheeky homage
To fine-lady piety
Posed in the purple toga.

The statue of Tommy Cooper in Caerphilly
Is telling jokes only you can hear,
Which is why you seem to be laughing wildly
Beside the straight-faced professor of philosophy,
Whose arm is politely around your shoulders;
The castle is background for your long curls
Lifted by a spirited breeze
And history is suddenly lyrical.

Relaxed, your head back over the stern
Of the boat I am rowing across the lake
Where ducks ate crumbs I flung when I was three,
Your eyes look so directly at me
That I know why I first fell in love with the world.

ONCE UPON A TIME

King Norm's wife's sister
Disturbed the just order
By failing to worship her husband
Sufficiently to discount the drink,
The beatings, other women.

Single again, not ordinary,
She lived where streets opened
On rough paths out to woods
And moors beyond mortgages,
A threat by sisterly example.

King Norm never beat his wife,
Kept his beer quiet in the shed,
His gambling hidden in the wardrobe,
Observing all the protocols
Laid down by God and money.

His was a modest kingdom,
Everything in place. Disharmony
Was rare and at its worst
His wife might say she'd have
A night out with her sister.

He feared the siblings shared
Some aberrant gene,
Though over two decades
His wife's sister's different life
Brought home no disapproval.

Not long before his unexpected death
King Norm changed unaccountably
And took pleasure in driving
With the beautiful sisters
For afternoon tea in Scarborough.

MUDDY WATERS: CLARKSDALE TO HULL

A summer afternoon slows into evening,
Lazy sunlight, heavy and warm,
Bringing out the red deep in the grain
Of rough-hewn cypress beams stacked and jointed
To form the walls of a four-square shack.

The young man sitting on the doorstep
Playing bottle-neck glissando on his guitar
Is tired from driving a tractor all day
In cotton fields that cover the miles
To the Mississippi oxbows where the sun goes down.

Ten years later, he's in Chicago,
Where the blues go north looking for work
When machines take over on the plantations
And the clubs and bars can't contain his music
That spills on records across the Atlantic

To bring him to Hull in 1968
For another crowd of long-haired white kids
Whose tastes in music worry their parents
To tap the deep pulse of the Delta
That's issuing from this man of fifty-three.

Later he's relaxed for an interview
With an inept hippy who wants to know
His opinion of the Rolling Stones,
Which makes him laugh, like a good joke
About how far he's come from Clarksdale.

LOVE AMONG THE PARTIALLY DEAF
IN OTLEY

When you told me in the dark
While asthma, sweat, and panic
Held me paused on one elbow
In my groping search
On the wooden couch
For comfort on the wooden slats,
Having left you there
In the too-small bed,
When you told me then,
Not afterwards
When I was up again
Alone and saw dawn
Seeping scarlet
Through a slash
in the heavy sky
Out to the level east,
Not then, but not long after
We'd passed in the dark
For the bathroom,
When *a propos* of nothing
You told me "I love you"
And I said "what's that?
Speak up!", so you did
As you said it again
And everything was suddenly in its place
And I said "Thank you" and fell asleep.

SCREAMER WOOD

December and the skeletal birches
In dense recessions give sufficient shade
To keep the puddles on the path frozen.

The day darkens and the soles of the feet
Register collapse in the fractile veins
Of ice crystals in mud and rotting leaves.

You're far in now, pathless, acres beyond
The last of the fly-tippers' fat black bags,
Rough reckoning the way home by sunset's West.

Fingers going white, feet numb, reluctant,
Breathing's shallow from forcing past panic
Through briars and the wreckage of fallen trees.

Your single pen must now refuse to write,
So take a couple of photos – trees and air – ,
Let twenty minutes get you out of there.

PRIVATE ROBERT EVANS, BURMA, 1944

When Evans went missing in the jungle
we had him down as a goner when
two of the others who'd vanished got back
after meeting up on the run from Japs.

The show was wonderful, Vera on stage
in searchlight beams with coloured lights
in the trees and the best rum ration since Christmas.
We cheered our hearts out, wouldn't let her stop.

She kept on singing while her make-up ran
with sweat and tears at all she had to give
to men four years away from home,
her white cliffs Sehnsucht resurrecting hope,

till a big shell exploded in the air
over the stage. Instant bloody chaos –
at least four dead, ten badly hit,
men staggering blinded with concussion.

The stage was wrecked and no sign of Vera.
I thought she'd copped it and they'd hushed it up,
till a few days later a bloke from Signals
told me she'd done a big show near Kohima.

We last saw Evans down near the stage
so thought he must have wandered off in shock.
For three days we drew lots for search parties,
then business-as-usual till three weeks later

when they found him crawling out of the jungle
through the mud slick down behind the latrines
and raving in malaria delirium
about *Vera*, *bamboo shoots*, *water*, the Japs.

He was in a coma for nearly a week,
then he'd shake all over, yelling Run, Vera, run!
and he only just made it, tough as he was,
with never another word about Vera.

She saw him, though, when her 'plane home stopped
near the field hospital. A bloke who knew him
swore that he heard her whispering to Evans,
"Thanks, Bob, we'll meet again some sunny day".

[Adapted from Lynne's Dad's wartime experiences.]

JUNE 2010

There they are, the rags on sticks,
 Durable tatters, colour gone
With years of weather,
 Marking ways to forgotten places.

Buoyant on sadness, slow piano music
 Is light moving on the water of morning.
 Here comes England, with its fraying flags
 Clipped to the Ford's back doors
 And the cut-price Carling from the cash-and-carry
 On the Wootton Bassett trading estate.

The absolute light on the cherry tree
 Blossoming above its neglected patch
 Gets lost in the purple twilight
 And disappears for days into thin rain.

UNDER NEW MANAGEMENT

On the day that Al Fayad sold Harrods,
You are among the tourists who come
To stroll through its halls without wishing to buy,
Extras in a production about bigger money
Than most of us call disposable income.

You turn the tag clipped to a handbag-
A colourful affair with slashed-satin flowers-
And murmur amazement to your companion
At a price that could feed a family for a year
Here are silk scarves and good ones for £600.

Diamond rings at eight for a million
Repose under immaculate glass
And intricate lighting set to enhance
Their sparkling's primal brilliance,
With similar, larger items, prices above display.

Feel free to proceed at your leisure.
Return, if you like, to the food hall
To inhale another heedful of the scent-
Essence of woodland, humus on heat-
Rising from baskets of exotic fungi.

Ride the Egyptian Escalator all the way up and down
Concede its big budget merits,
Its fine disclosure of successive floors
Abundant with marvellous things that enrich
Your catalogue of what money can buy.

It's a shop. People go there, many, like you,
To swell scenes with a few star purchases,
Some of whom must be present somewhere among
Those drifting in and out on the day
When ownership passes to the Emirate of Quatar.

AFORE YE GO…

Think where man's glory most begins and ends,
And say my glory was I had such friends. – WB Yeats

Farewell e-learning colleagues. Time to go.
The application's closing down. The plot
Is lost, become a pear-shaped tale of woe
That ends not in a bang but with slow rot
Beneath a heap of finest HR fudge,
While management proceeds without a clue
And asks when meeting each redundant drudge
'Before you leave, please tell us what to do'.

I'm off, the first to go, must take my leave
Of you lot with whom working was such fun.
To that extent I have good cause to grieve,
But I'll be OK out there on the run
Into the future where the next gig waits
Beyond the fog that's settled on us here
As ECW disintegrates.
Good luck my friends; redundancy draws near.